D0934182

Chicken Soup for the Soul®
Heartwarming Stories to
Renew Your Faith

**Andrews McMeel
Publishing**

Kansas City

Library of Congress Card Catalog Number: 99-62880

ISBN: 0-7407-0121-5

Chicken Soup for the Soul®
Heartwarming Stories to Renew Your Faith

Inspired by the #1 *New York Times* bestseller

by Jack Canfield and Mark Victor Hansen

Great Love

by Michael Peterson

I n the winter of 1990, I was asked to appear on a television talk show in Toronto, Ontario, Canada. At the end of our first day of taping I was on my way back to my plush, high-rise, cable-TV, twenty-four-hour room service hotel, when I saw something I'd never seen before.

Lying on the sidewalk against a building in four inches of snow was a man sleeping with only a cardboard blanket to keep him from being completely exposed to the freezing cold. What really broke my heart was when I realized that he wore no shoes or socks.

I thought to stop and help him but was not quite sure what to do. As the traffic light turned green, it seemed life was demanding that I move along. So I did. Back in the "anything I wanted was mine" environment of my hotel, I promptly forgot about the man on the street.

Several days later, prior to the morning taping, I was having coffee and Danish in the green room at the station. All of the "important" people had left the room and it was just me and the janitor remaining.

I had seen him quietly go about his business every day while I was there, and he never said a word except "Good morning" or "Can I get anything for you, sir?" He always had a smile to give to everyone. When I asked him how he was feeling today, he told me that he'd been having to ride his bike to work in the snow and that he'd been feeling rather sorry for himself . . . that is, until he saw a man sleeping down on the corner of Yonge

Street and Bloor with just a piece of cardboard for covering from the cold and no
shoes. I almost choked on my Danish as I
heard him go on to relate how he was so
moved with compassion for the man that he
went around the corner to a store and bought
the man a pair of socks and shoes.

As I heard his story, I saw in my mind a
poster that used to be in an old friend's bed-
room when I was a teenager. It was a picture
of a child handing someone a flower and the
caption read: "The smallest deed always
exceeds the grandest of intentions."

I stood there wishing it was me who had
bought the shoes and socks for the man,
when they called my name to come to the set.

As I got to the studio, they were just con-
cluding an interview with a social worker who

specialized in benevolence for eastern Ontario. The social worker relayed a story about Mother Teresa, who when asked once how she had accomplished such great things in her life responded, "None of us can do anything great on our own, but we can all do a small thing with great love."

When I went home that day, I looked for the man on the street. He was gone, but I knew it wouldn't be long before someone took his place.

What Color Are You?

by Melissa D. Strong Eastham

A s a second-grade teacher in an inner-city school, I am often faced with the task of answering questions that really have nothing to do with our course of study for the day—questions that you won't find on any national standardized tests. Some of these questions can be recycled into research for the class ("Mrs. Eastham, why are butterflies all different colors?" "How does the grass die in the winter and then come alive in the spring?") Others are much more ponderous and may not have an exact right or wrong answer.

Since I am not one to squelch curiosity, we often take these opportunities as they arise and have short class discussions on them. I let everyone comment on the subject and then tell them we can each make up our own minds. ("Why do we have homework *every night?*" "Are there really such things as angels?")

Our discussion on differences started innocently enough. I asked the class if they could tell me whether a very tall man was good or bad. They agreed that you couldn't tell if someone was good or bad just because they were tall. I told them that I knew someone who couldn't walk well and so she rode in a wheelchair most of the time. I asked if that person was bad or mean because she uses a wheelchair, and they all agreed that you couldn't tell. We went on for a while in this vein and came to the conclusion that being different doesn't make someone good or bad, it just makes that person different.

I decided to take the discussion to a more personal level and explore our personal differences. We talked about how we are all different from one another, how no two people are exactly alike, how even twins have different personalities or features that define them as individuals. I went on to tell them that I was different from everyone in the room because I was the tallest. I was also different because I lived in Red Oak and everyone else lived in Dallas.

Then I planned to have each of them tell the class how they were different. But before I could call on the first pupil, my quietest student raised his hand and announced, "Mrs. Eastham is different because she is a different color."

As I think back now, I realize that if this

had been said in a room with fifteen other adults, this simple statement of truth would have laid out on the floor, floundering like a fish out of water, while embarrassed glances waited for someone to break the awkward silence. Not so in a classroom of fifteen second-graders. They jumped on it!

"Yeah, Mrs. Eastham is white."

"No, she's not, she's peach!"

"I think she's really just bright brown."

"She's creamy."

"She's kinda yellow."

"She's just really shiny."

Trying to hide my grin, I told the class they could have small group discussions on it while I turned the attendance report into the office. I barely made it out of the room before my smirk turned into a full belly laugh. I chuckled all the way to the office and related the story to a fellow teacher while there. I couldn't wait to get back to the room to hear them discuss this!

When I opened the door, they were already back in their seats. They had finished their discussion. (Darn, I had missed it!) I picked a spokesperson for the group, and he said that they knew what color I was but they wanted me to tell them if they were right or not. I said that since this question had only one right answer, I would tell them if they had guessed right or not. Then he told me that the class had decided that I was clear.

Clear? Somehow I was able to suppress my laughter. How did they come up with *that?* I was saved by the bell, as it was time for them to go to gym. I told them we could talk about it after gym and sent them on their way. Looking back now, I know *someone* was looking out for me.

While grading papers, I began to muse over our morning again. I was reminded of the times I had been at conferences and workshops and even dinner parties and had been asked, "How many of your students are black? How many white children are in your class? Do you teach many Hispanics?" So many times I have had to stop and try to count out the answers. "How many black students do I have? I know I have fifteen kids. Is it ten black and five Hispanic, or eleven and four?"

The person posing the question is very

often amazed and perplexed that I don't know the ethnic makeup of my classroom. I guess it's because when I am teaching, I am teaching children, not colors. I began to realize that it was the same for my kids. They don't see me as black or white or Hispanic; they see me as a person, someone who cares about them, encourages them to do their best and works hard with them every day.

When my students got back to the room, they were all still abuzz about our morning discussion and begged me to tell them if they were right or wrong. I had to tell them the truth. They were exactly right. I am *clear!*

Now when I am asked that inevitable question at dinner parties or conventions or workshops — "How many black and Hispanic and white children do you have?" — I have a pat answer that works every time, with no fumbling or counting. I look the person straight in the eye and say, "None. They are all clear."

21

Medicine

by Jeanne Morris

In September of the year that my second child was born, my husband and I moved from a small town to a large city. We were young and had no money, so we rented a mobile home and parked in the woods just outside the city limits. All too soon my son Steve was born, several weeks early and weighing under four pounds. Such tiny babies require special and very expensive care. With the huge hospital bill added to the cost of moving, I wondered how we could ever repay the enormous debt. But I knew that with God's help we would manage somehow.

Our new home was small and isolated but I loved it. The trees were flaunting their glorious colors and our only neighbors were

chipmunks and raccoons. I even loved the
long walks to the store, although it was a mile
to the main road, half a mile farther to the
pay telephone and another half-mile to the
store, making a round trip of four miles. I
would put my babies in the stroller and set off
on an adventure to buy milk and bread, never
knowing what wild birds or small animals we
might see along the way.

One morning in early December, I woke
up to a new world. During the night a sudden
snowstorm had transformed our woods into a
magic delight, where billowing drifts of deep
snow completely covered the fences and
glittering ice crystals spangled the trees. I
hurried to wake up my children and show
them the beauty of winter. My two-year-old
daughter, Evelyn, was awake and eager to get

dressed, but when I touched my tiny son he was burning with fever.

With sudden fear, I realized just how isolated we were. We had no phone, we were over two miles from the nearest person who might help, and, even worse, our dirt road was on private property; the snow plows would not come.

It was not possible to carry two children through such deep drifts of snow. If only I had a sled or a toboggan to take them to a bus stop; if only my husband were here; if only the buses were running; if only... It was not possible to take my baby to the doctor. There was nothing I could do. I felt the knot of fear pulling tighter and tighter in the pit of my stomach.

I knelt to pray. "Dear Lord," I said, "please

help me. I am so afraid for my baby and I don't know what to do." As I waited for an answer, I began to realize that I was seeing the problem the wrong way. It wasn't necessary to take the baby to the doctor, it was only necessary to bring the doctor's knowledge and medicine to the baby. I could telephone him and ask for a prescription for the right medicine. Reassured, I began to bundle up for the long trek to the phone. I was just pulling my boots on when I heard a knock at the door. I could not imagine who it might be. The only person who knew we were there was my husband, and he was out of town. I opened the door, and to my amazement I saw the man who delivered milk to the convenience store down the road. I didn't know his name, but I had seen him there several times and had spoken to him once or twice in passing. He smiled and said, "Hi, need any milk?"

Speechless I nodded and opened the door wide to let him in. He continued, "I almost didn't come to work today, it's such a mess out there." He waved his arm to include the woods, the snow and the highway beyond. "But I couldn't stop thinking about you and those babies away back here with no milk, so I decided to deliver to the little store anyway. Then I thought I might as well bring it the rest of the way since it wasn't much farther. Mind you, it's farther than I thought with the snow so deep and all. It kind of wore me out. I hope you don't mind if I sit and rest a minute before I start back."

I poured him a cup of coffee and made sure he was comfortable. Then I told him about the baby and finished by saying, "I know that you are the answer to my prayer. If you will stay with the children while I phone the doctor, I won't need to worry. I was afraid to leave them alone, but until you came, I thought I had no choice."

He thought about it for a minute, nodded and said, "I couldn't leave them alone either. You had best get started." He smiled and added, "I'm glad I broke a trail for you."

As I closed the door behind me, I heard Evelyn say her favorite words, "Read to me?"

Even with a trail broken it took me almost an hour to reach the road, with much slipping and falling. I was exhausted by the time I reached the telephone. But the Lord was with me. I reached the doctor on the first try. He remembered the baby and realized at once that this was a serious condition for such a fragile infant. By careful questioning he determined that Steve had an ear infection. He assured me that modern antibiotics would quickly bring this infection under control.

"But," he warned, "you must give it to him as soon as you can. Tomorrow might be too late.

"So," he explained, "I will call the pharmacy and tell them to prepare it for you right away. This is something new and it is quite expensive, but I think in this case it is necessary. What is the name of the nearest pharmacy?"

I told him the name of a large company I had seen in a shopping center several miles away and added, "How much do you think it will cost?"

He named a price so high I was stunned. *Where in the world could I get that much money?* I stammered my thanks and hung up the phone while my mind raced, attempting to discover a way.

I didn't know anyone in the city. I looked in the directory and called several charities, but they all seemed to have the same requirement. Each time I was told, "Come downtown and fill out an application, then we'll see if you qualify. If you feel that you can't wait, take the child to the county hospital." Where? On the other side of town, of course.

By this time I was ready to panic. I only had one coin left for the phone and I still had no idea where to get the money or what to do. Then it occurred to me that there was a way to get the medicine without paying for it. I could wait until the store closed, break in the back door and steal the medicine. I couldn't get the wrong one since it would have my baby's name on it.

I had never stolen anything before. I knew stealing was a sin, something God had specifically commanded us not to do. But I had to get the medicine if my baby was to survive. Surely God would forgive me.

I prayed, "Dear Lord, please guide me. I don't want to steal, but I have tried everything, and there is no other way."

Then I heard a voice, as calm and clear as if someone was standing beside me.

The voice said, "Unless they give it to you…"

Give it to me? The idea was so ridiculous I almost laughed out loud. But I only said: "Yes,

Lord, I will ask them."

I did not believe for one minute that a large drugstore would give an expensive medicine to a total stranger, but until I asked them, I could not say honestly that I had tried everything.

So I used my last coin and I called the drugstore. When the pharmacist answered, I told him who I was and asked if he had received a prescription from my doctor. He confirmed the order and added that it was ready. I took a deep breath and prepared myself for rejection.

"You don't know me," I said, "but I live a few miles away in a trailer parked on Sovereign Road. I don't have any money but my baby is very sick. If you would let me have the medicine now I will pay you when I can."

The pharmacist said, "That's fine. Can you pick it up or would you like us to deliver it?"

"You can deliver it?" I asked in astonishment.

"Oh yes," he replied. "We have a young man here who came to work today in a Jeep with four-wheel drive. I wondered why he brought the Jeep today, but now I know."

"Thank God!" I cried.

"Yes," the pharmacist agreed. "We do that here quite often." After I thanked him and hung up the phone, I just stood there, hip deep in snow, filled with awe and wonder, and praising God. I believe I had just experienced what is called "Amazing Grace."

This was the first time I was aware of God's hand on my life, but it was certainly not the last. I did not have an easy road to travel, but every time I reached the point where trouble was so deep that I thought I could go no farther, someone came along to help me through the deepest drifts. I didn't always know who these people were, but I always knew who sent them.

The Favorite Vase

by Belladonna Richuitti, age12

My younger brother and I were home watching cartoons while my father slept and my mother was out shopping. I left my brother in the living room and went to get something to drink. As I was pouring some orange juice, I heard something break. First, I looked in to see if my father had woken up, and he hadn't. Then I quickly ran to see what had happened. When I went into the living room, I was shocked. My brother had broken my mother's favorite vase.

"What did you do?" I gasped.

"I broke it!" my brother answered. "It was an accident!"

Knowing that he was freaked out, and not wanting him to get in trouble, I did what any friend would do. I tried to help him. I quickly ran and got some glue. I didn't know what time my mother was going to be back or when my father was going to wake up, so I tried to hurry. I frantically gathered up all of the broken pieces and started to glue them together. It took me an hour but I *finally* fixed the vase. Then came the real disaster.

"Oh my gawd! Oh my gawd!" I screamed.

I had fixed the vase, but I had accidentally glued my hair to it!

While my brother looked at me like I was some kind of idiot, I carried the vase—with my hair attached to it—into the bathroom. I looked in the mirror.

"My beautiful hair," I cried. Realizing that there was no way to pull my hair from the vase, I grabbed a pair of scissors. With every single strand of hair that I cut, I cried again. My hair was ruined and the vase looked like a wig was attached to it! As I was leaving the bathroom with my ridiculous new hairdo, I heard a key turn in the front door. "Hey guys, I'm back!"

My mother was back! My brother ran to his room and quickly pretended to be asleep leaving me to deal with her all by myself. Before I could explain, my mother yelled at me and grounded me because she thought I had broken the vase. I went to my room to think about what had happened. I was grounded and I was also going to have to go to school looking like an idiot!

While I was lying on my bed looking up at the ceiling, I realized that what I had done for my brother was an act of friendship. I knew that even though my brother and I fight a lot, I had made a sacrifice for him. This was a huge sacrifice though — my hair and my freedom!

"Knock, knock," sounded someone at my door.

"Who is it?" I asked.

My brother walked in and gave me a hug.

"Thank you," he said.

"You're welcome," I replied. "I guess that's what a big sister is for, to be a friend when you need one."

Consider This

by Jack Canfield &
Mark Victor Hansen

Consider this:

Robert Frost, one of the greatest poets that America has produced, labored for twenty years without fame or success. He was thirty-nine years old before he sold a single volume of poetry. Today his poems have been published in some twenty-two languages and he won the Pulitzer Prize for poetry four times.

Albert Einstein, often said to be the smartest person who has ever lived, is quoted as saying, "I think and think for months and years. Ninety-nine times the conclusion is false. The hundredth time I am right."

By the end of World War II, prominent CBS newsman William Shirer had decided that he wanted to write professionally. During the next twelve years he was consumed with his writing. Unfortunately, his books rarely sold, and he often had difficulty feeding his family. Out of this period, however, came a manuscript that was 1,200 pages long. Everyone—his agent, his editor, his publisher, his friends—told him it would never sell because of its length. And when Shirer finally did get it published, it was priced at ten dollars, the most expensive book of its time. No one expected it to be of any interest except to scholars. But *The Rise and Fall of the Third Reich* made publishing history. Its first printing sold out completely on the first day. Even today it remains the all-time biggest seller in the history of the Book-of-the-Month Club.

When Luciano Pavarotti graduated from college, he was unsure of whether he should become a teacher or a professional singer. His father told him, "Luciano, if you try to sit in two chairs, you will fall between them. You must choose one chair." Pavarotti chose singing. It took seven more years of study and frustration before he made his first professional appearance, and it took another seven years before he reached the Metropolitan Opera. But he had chosen his chair and had become successful.

When Enrico Caruso, the great Italian tenor, took his first voice lesson, the instructor pronounced him hopeless. He said his voice sounded like wind whistling through a window.

Walt Disney was once fired by a newspaper editor for lack of imagination. Disney recalled his early days of failure: "When I was nearly twenty-one years old I went broke for the first time. I slept on cushions from an old sofa and ate cold beans out of a can."

Scottie Pippen, who won four NBA championship rings and two Olympic gold medals, received no athletic scholarship from any university and originally made his small college basketball team as the equipment manager.

Gregor Mendel, the Austrian botanist whose experiments with peas originated the modern science of genetics, never even succeeded in passing the examination to become a high school science teacher. He failed biology.

Henry Ford forgot to put a reverse gear in the first car he invented. He also didn't build a door wide enough to get the car out of the building he built it in. If you go to Greenfield

Village, you can see where he cut a hole in the wall to get the car out.

Dr. Benjamin Bloom of the University of Chicago conducted a five-year study of leading artists, athletes and scholars based on anonymous interviews with the top twenty performers in various fields, as well as with their friends, families and teachers. He wanted to discover the common characteristics of these achievers that led to their tremendous successes. "We expected to find tales of great natural gifts," Bloom commented. "We didn't find that at all. Their mothers often said it was another child who had the greater talents." What they did find were accounts of extreme hard work and dedication: the swimmer who performed laps for two hours every morning before school and the pianist who practiced several hours a day for seventeen years. Bloom's research determined conclusively that drive, determination and hard work — not great talent — were what led these individuals to their extraordinary achievements.

Artur Rubinstein once astounded a young inquirer with the statement that he practiced piano eight hours a day, every day of his life. "But, sir!" exclaimed the young man. "You are so good. Why do you practice so much?"

"I wish to become superb," replied the master pianist.

A study of elite violinists showed that the number of hours spent practicing was the only factor that separated potential music superstars from others who were merely good. Following the careers of violinists studying at the Music Academy of West Berlin, psychologists found that by the time the students were eighteen, the best musicians had already spent, on average, about 2,000 more hours in practice than their fellow students.

A visitor once told Michelangelo, "I can't see that you have made any progress since I was here the last time." Michelangelo answered, "Oh, yes, I have made much progress. Look carefully and you will see that I have retouched this part, and that I have polished that part. See, I have worked on this part, and have softened lines here."

"Yes," said the visitor, "but those are all trifles."

"That may be," replied Michelangelo, "but trifles make perfection and perfection is no trifle."

One of the most beautiful speaking voices

on stage and screen belongs to James Earl Jones. Did you know that Jones has long battled a severe stuttering problem? From age nine until his mid-teens he had to communicate with teachers and classmates by handwritten notes. A high school English teacher gave him the help he needed, but he still struggles with his problem to this day. Yet there is no finer speaking voice than his. He was recently listed among the ten actors with the most beautiful speaking voice.

Charles Darwin spent most of his adult life in pain, suffering from one mysterious ailment after another. Yet he made immeasurable contributions to the study of the origins of life.

Born prematurely and left in the care of his grandparents, Sir Isaac Newton was taken out of school early and became an inept farm boy.

Now he is considered one of the greatest figures in the entire history of science.

Paul Galvin created Motorola out of the ashes of his own bankrupt company. In 1928 Galvin was able to piece together enough money to buy back a small division of a company he had owned that was on the auction block. From that division he built Motorola, a Fortune 500 company that has been highly successful.

The Guinness Book of World Records records the true story of a man who ate an entire bicycle, tires and all! But he didn't eat it all at once. Over a period of seventeen days, from March 17 to April 2, 1977, Michel Lotito of Grenoble, France, melted the parts into small swallowable units and consumed every piece.

George MacDonald once noted that one

draft horse can move two tons of weight. However, two draft horses in harness, working together, can move twenty-three tons of weight.

53

Daddy's Little Girl

by Kippi Brannon

When I heard the song "Daddy's Little Girl," every line in the lyrics related to me. Daddy was a very big influence in my life. Besides teaching me a good work ethic, he also influenced me musically—he taught me how to play the guitar. In spite of our closeness throughout my childhood and in our relationship today, Daddy never really showed a lot of physical affection towards me. As a former Marine, showing emotion and hugging was never something that came easy to him. He always demonstrated his love by working hard, giving me encouragement to be a good person and providing for me.

All that changed the night of June 12, 1997. I was scheduled to do a Father's Day show on

TNN's *Primetime Country,* and the producers wanted my father to be with me as part of the program. They had asked me to sing my song, "Daddy's Little Girl," and then do the normal interview portion with Gary Chapman and my dad. The interview segment was going to be a piece of cake, I thought, because I love to talk! However, the performance portion was creating real anxiety for me—not only because it would be my first time singing the song in front of my father, but sixteen years had passed since the last time he and I had hugged or said, "I love you."

So the big moment finally arrived. With just thirty seconds until I had to perform, I stepped from behind the curtain and onto the stage. There, in the front row of the auditorium, sat my dad.

As the piano introduction started, I could tell Daddy was fighting back the tears. I felt the professional thing to do was be tough and try to rise above the emotion I was feeling, but there was no way! The more I sang, the more sensitive I became. Overwhelmed, I heard my voice start cracking while uncontrollable sobs accompanied each line. As I got ready to sing the last verse, I saw that Daddy had tears streaming down his face. I just lost it! I walked into the audience to share Daddy's embrace as I sang through the ending of the song.

All those years without an "I love you" or a hug were all redeemed for us that night right there on national TV as millions of viewers shared that priceless moment.

Baby's Ears

by Valerie Allen

Mom poured herself a glass of orange juice. "I'm worried about Grandma," she said. I was pouring syrup on my French toast, hot and sweet, just the way I liked it.

"Why?" I asked as I licked a drop of syrup from my fork.

"Well, remember before she moved to Florida, how early Grandma would get up?"

"Before the sun," I said, "to make pancakes and bacon."

My mom nodded. "But now Grandma sleeps most of the day or watches television. I can't get her out of the house, and she won't try to make friends." Mom frowned and lowered her voice. "Grandma's even talking about going back to New York."

"Back to New York? But you said that she

couldn't live alone anymore. That's why she came to live here." I like Florida. Of course, I have a lot of girlfriends to play with in my sixth-grade class.

"If Grandma went back to New York, she would have to live in a nursing home," my mother told me. "That's a place where old people live and nurses take care of them."

"It sounds like a hospital to me," I said. I thought for a minute. "I'll find a way to make Grandma like Florida."

Mom smiled and said, "I wish you could."

After school, I saw Grandma watching television and figured she hadn't moved all day. In my room, I sat on my bed and took out my seashell collection. I had found Striped Whelks, Purple Sea Snails and even a Queen Conch Shell. You can hold a conch shell up to

your ear and actually hear the ocean waves.
My very favorite shell was called a Baby's Ear.
It's a beautiful white shell shaped just like the
ear of a baby, all swirly and delicate.

Looking at my seashells gave me an idea.
I went into the living room and sat on the
couch. "Did you ever go to the beach when
you were little, Grandma?" I asked.

"Once my mother took me, but I didn't
enjoy it at all," she said, frowning.

"Really?" I took an oatmeal cookie from
the plate on the coffee table. "Why not?"

"I'm afraid of the water, and I can't swim."
Grandma pursed her lips as though she'd
tasted a lemon. I wished Grandma could feel
the way I did about the beach. I loved to see
pelicans flying over the water, and once I even
saw a huge green iguana.

"Well, I was wondering if you could take me to the beach, Grandma. I need some new shells for my collection."

Grandma didn't even look up from the TV. "I'm watching my show, Val. Can't you go by yourself?"

"No. I'm not allowed to go to the beach by myself. Please!" I begged, imagining Grandma in a nursing home.

"Oh, all right," Grandma sighed. She took my hand as we left the house, and we walked to the beach. The sun felt hot enough to melt metal. I handed Grandma a plastic bag. "Here. This is for the seashells you find."

"Oh, I'll leave that to you," she said. A soft ocean breeze blew her gray curls across her eyes.

I shook my head. "No, Grandma. I need all the help I can get."

"Oh, all right," she said. We walked side by side up the beach, our heads down, looking for only the most beautiful shells.

"Doesn't look like there's much to choose from," Grandma said, shading her eyes with her hand. "Maybe we should go home."

"Not yet, Grandma! I'll go ahead like a scout and see if I find anything good." I looked back at her as I walked ahead. Grandma stood watching the ocean waves and the seagulls that flew over the water searching for fish. She took off her shoes and carried them.

I ran on ahead and slipped a Pink Triton shell from my pocket, dropping it in the sand. Farther up the beach, I did the same with my Blue Starfish and my Green Serpent Star. Finally, I dropped my favorite shell, the Baby's Ear.

Just then, I heard Grandma shout, "Val!

Look what I found!" Grandma stood in the sand, holding up the pink Triton.

"That's beautiful, Grandma!" I cried. "It will look great in my collection."

Grandma nodded and smiled. "Let's keep looking!" she said, suddenly excited. I pretended to pass right by the Blue Starfish, but Grandma bent down slowly and picked it up. "Val! Look at this starfish. It's blue!"

"You're really good at this, Grandma!"

She carried her plastic bag proudly. At last, Grandma came to my favorite shell.

"Val, look at this strange thing." She handed it to me.

I cradled the shell in my hand. "It's called a Baby's Ear because that's what it looks like."

"You're pretty good at this yourself, Val," Grandma said, giving me a hug. On the way home we waded in the ocean. Grandma seemed to have forgotten her fear of water.

We met my mom on the front porch. "We've been to the beach," Grandma told her. "And you know, I think I'll start a shell collection of my own. You can help me, Val."

"Okay, Grandma," I said.

My mom and I shared a secret smile.

Rodeo Joe

by James C. Brown, M.D.

David was a nine-year-old who had an unusual form of cancer involving the muscle of his leg. He was diagnosed at the age of eight and underwent major surgical excision. He was now on a continual regime of chemotherapy. The surgery had left him with significant weakening of his left leg and a noticeable limp, but he was otherwise disease-free. I was told by his parents that he was still the best worker on their little North Carolina farm. David's favorite chores involved attending to his horse and best friend, Rodeo Joe. As the staff became acquainted with David and his family, we also learned all about Rodeo Joe. Joe was a twenty-five-year-old quarter horse who in his day had been a talented cow horse, and who now in his retirement had become the best friend of a nine-year-old farm boy.

At age ten, David returned to the hospital with signs and symptoms suggesting that his disease had returned. Indeed it had, with a vengeance. There was local recurrence as well as involvement of the bone marrow, blood-stream and liver. David was very, very sick. Another round of chemotherapy was initiated, with full knowledge that the odds of a good response were minimal at best.

Chemotherapy often has negative effects on the body. As these potent substances are attacking tumor cells, they can also attack healthy, normal cells that we need for survival. Chemotherapy, in fact, can in and of itself be lethal. The balance one must obtain between too much and/or too little chemotherapy is indeed a delicate art form practiced by dedicated pediatric oncologists.

David's tumor and metastasis began to respond to the medicine, but unfortunately his immune system also became significantly impaired, and he soon developed infections involving his lungs and spinal fluid. David was a bright boy. He knew he was sick and that he may be dying. The weaker he became, the more he talked about Rodeo Joe. On our medical rounds, David would tell all of us about Joe's abilities with the cattle, and about all the ribbons he had won in his younger days. He would tell us how Joe knew when the school bus was coming and would be waiting at the fence. David would often jump on for a bareback fling around the pasture before doing his chores.

Gradually David became weaker and weaker. Soon he only grasped a well-worn photo of Rodeo Joe, which he would sometimes hold up to visitors. His only articulation to us became the repeated question, "Will I see Joe again? Can I ride him just one more time...just one more time?" The infection was so aggressive, it was difficult to control. David soon slipped into a coma. We doctors felt certain that the disease and infection were most likely too advanced, and that he would soon die.

David's parents were like most parents, totally devoted to their son. They were not wealthy people by any means, and the demands of their small farm by which they made their living did not cease. Caring neighbors lending a helping hand were a blessing, but Mr. and Mrs. Statler still divided their time between farm chores miles away and comforting their dying son in the hospital. They took little time to eat or sleep.

Three things stand out in my mind as I recall the time of David's coma. First is the resolute strength, determination and faith of the parents and their powerful love. Mr. Statler would say to me every day, "I do believe Davey will be ridin' that ol' gelding again, I believe he will." Next, I remember the hundreds of cards and letters taped up all over his room as David was being prayed for by a number of prayer groups all over the country. Finally, I can vividly recall all the pictures of that old horse, tacked up on the headboard of that pediatric bed. We all wanted David to ride that horse one more time. We hoped that he would come out of his coma long enough to at least see him, and we devised plans to haul Joe to the hospital grounds. We also all thought this was wishful thinking, as David's condition steadily worsened.

Then truly miraculously, for reasons not well understood by this physician, David's condition improved — and improved rapidly. The infections began to clear. David's own defense cells began to come back strong. Within forty-eight hours he was awake, alert and talking to us again about Rodeo Joe. Because of the extent of his cancer, we feared that this might only be temporary, so we wanted to try to get him home for at least one last ride with Joe. However, in running tests to evaluate the extent of the cancer, there was none to be found. Not in the leg, or in the liver, or in the spinal fluid.

One week later, David went back home to the farm, back with Rodeo Joe. A couple of months went by. I decided to go see David and his family and this old horse I had heard so much about.

It was a beautiful fall day in North Carolina, the multicolored leaves made brilliant by the bright October sun. Their little farm was just off a secondary highway and easy to find. As I turned into the drive, I saw Rodeo Joe standing under a large orange oak tree with David sitting on his back facing backward, brushing the horse's rump. David hadn't noticed me yet, and I could see he was talking to Joe. Maybe he was sharing the story about how the doctors didn't think he'd make it back to ride Joe, but how the two of them knew he would.

I sat for a few minutes trying to match this scene with the one in the hospital, trying to understand it all. I watched the cars driving by on the highway with their occupants noticing the young boy and horse under the tall oak. I had this urge to stop traffic and explain to these people that yes, this is a picturesque fall farm scene, but you are really seeing a miracle. A miracle! But I didn't; I simply sat and watched.

The Front-Row Seats

by Roxane Russell

My family have always been country music fans. My mother's favorite entertainer was Porter Wagoner, and even as a little girl of five growing up in Louisiana, Momma passed that "hero worship" on to me. While all of my friends were singing Beatles tunes, I knew all the words to "Slew Foot."

One of my earliest memories was the day Porter was to perform near my hometown at the Ponchatoula Hayride. We stood in line for four hours just waiting for the doors to open so we could get a good seat. Unfortunately, hundreds of other people had the same idea, and by the time Momma made it through the rushing crowd, protecting her small daughter, we had to sit near the back of the building. Instead of being disappointed, Momma smiled at me, took my hand and said, "That's okay, baby. One of these days we're going to have front-row seats."

As fate would have it, thirty years later I was the feature producer for the television program *Opry Backstage* on TNN. I can't begin to tell you how proud that made Momma. She had been suffering from an extended illness and died soon after I got the position. However, she died knowing I was working with the stars of her beloved Grand Ole Opry.

Shortly after her death my producer, Rusty Wilcoxen, asked me to participate in a live segment for the show. I was to be interviewed by the host of *Opry Backstage* — Porter Wagoner. During the commercial break as I was being miked and placed into position for the interview, I felt as if someone had taken my hand. No one was touching me, but the sensation was real.

As I looked at the crew in front of me, my thoughts suddenly raced to Momma, and for an instant I was the five-year-old girl again. To my left, less than a foot away, sat Momma's favorite entertainer about to talk to her only child in front of millions of viewers. A single tear trickled down my cheek. As the floor manager was counting us out of the break, I spoke to Momma. Not out loud, but from the heart.

We did it, Momma. We finally got those front-row seats! The tear was replaced by a smile.